LOUIE BOY

Gliding the Connections Between
Somewhere and Elsewhere

LOUIE BOY

Gliding the Connections Between
Somewhere and Elsewhere

Poems By
YCT VASSEL

Acknowledgment

To my mother, Ivy, who bought me books from her monthly paychecks that had numerous demands. Credit, or blame, also goes to my Fourth Form English teacher - Mrs. Judith Williams - who chose my very first attempt at a poem as an example for our class. Thanks also to the women of my Monday Writing Group - Valada, Debra, Francine, Sharon H, Ruth and Sharon M - whose love and generosity have sustained me. A curtsey also to Lynn O who has always shared her favorite poems, and to Joan who reads, encourages, loves my poems and loves me.

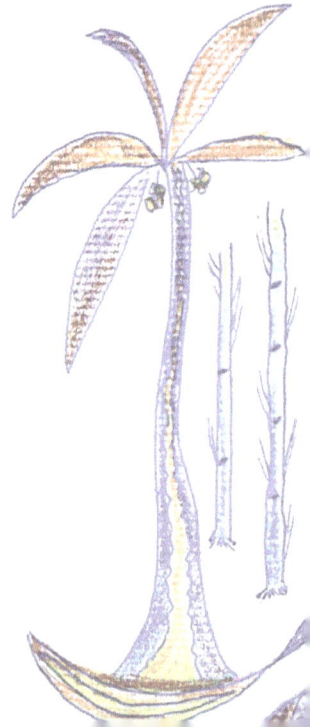

Artwork courtesy of Joan E. Nelson

Guerrilla Man

(Circa 1980 for a college writing class)

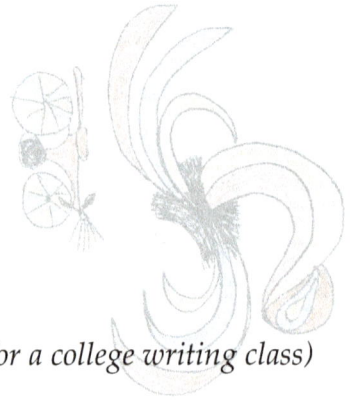

I heard he died last Saturday noon
Killed by a shotgun blast as
Fruit he bought by a wayside stand.

Seems the man didn't like his looks
Nor his car
Or the way he spoke.

Neil, he tried to beat down the price
On a bag oranges
But didn't know golden fruit
Would spill his blood
To be dried by old gold sun.

Seems the man then shot up the car
(stupid jack, he coulda driven it off)
Then took to bush screaming he'd
Rid the land of all 'talists.

In days to come
From the trees he'll aim and
Bring them down for crows
To feast.

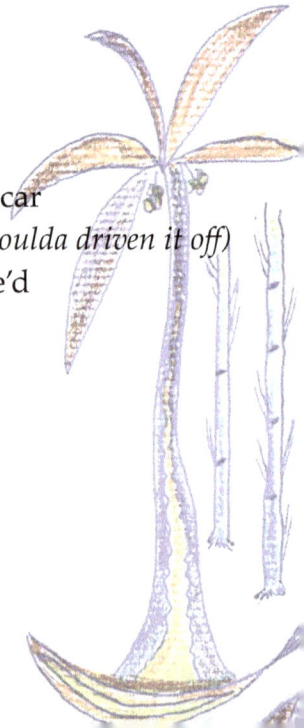

No more fancy cars to ride beside
The barefoot man.

No more shacks being washed
Down river by friendly drizzles.

No more walking through garbage
To find an evening meal.

No. No more!

In the vision of a
Perfect creation
He'll come with his people behind
A gun in hand 'stead of flute
Down from the mountains
Out from the trees
Cheers and tears and laughter
And music
Marking the way to the sea
Where in face of the horizon
A new future he'll proclaim.

Yes
I heard he died
Last Saturday noon
Killed by a shotgun blast
In face of the horizon.

For Joan, my love

Table of Contents

FIVE   91

EPILOGUE   94

ABOUT THE AUTHOR   97

PUBLICATION ACKNOWLEDGMENT   98

LOUIE BOY

Gliding the Connections Between
Somewhere and Elsewhere

One

Spaceship Earth

(Circa 1970s After Reading the Book)

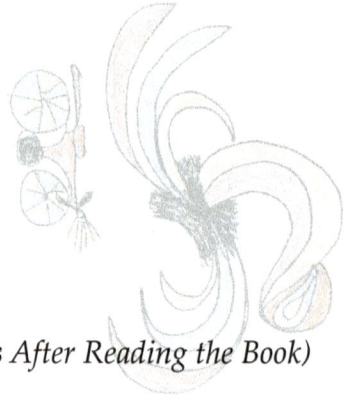

Travelling together through
Time and space
Living together
Working together
On our spaceship earth
Springing from loins
Created by the genius
Of our god

Time passes
Meaning nothing
Fallen leaves feed
The trees
Souls leave and are
Born again
The earth moves
Yet remains

And so travelers we
Will be
Remaining here
Going where?
No one knows
But our god
Looking down on
Spaceship earth

Louie Boy

(Tribute to my friend Joey who was dying of AIDS)

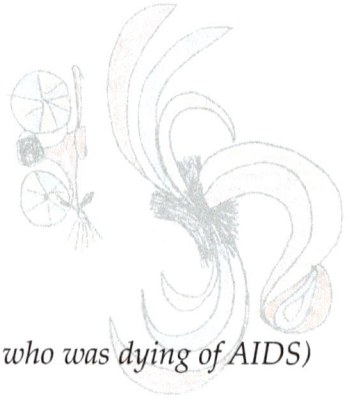

Once I saw a train pass by
With the words *Louie Boy*
Splashed in yellow upon
Its red side

Yellow and red are my
Colors for you
Yellow for sunshine
Red for the passion of a
Courage smoldering deep

Trains and dreams glide on
Tracks connected to obscure
Stations
One of life's fragments
Set before us
For a nicer view

We observe then forget
For waking dreams are still
Just dreams with no beginnings
And so, no ends

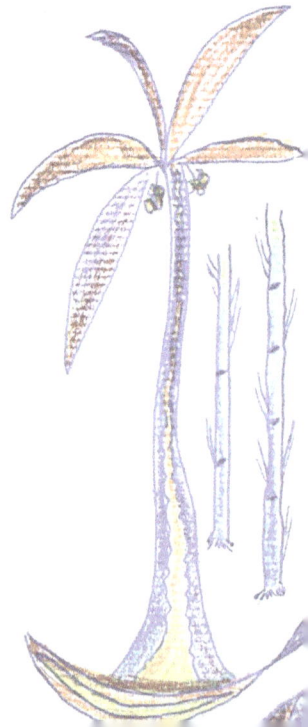

Where is the notice for
Small moments
Unless it's splashed
With colors screaming

Here is a tribute to a friend
Be he fragment or a boxcar on
Clattering wheels
Gliding the connections
Between somewhere and elsewhere

He'll be remembered for the
Yellow
Of the sun that lights
The red of embers
Glowing
For Louie
Louie Boy

Once We Were Children

Once we were children
      looking to the future as an
            endless world of bright blue skies
                and sun-washed landscapes
For we could be anything and
      anyone in this blue, blue world
          of our dreamtime wanderings.

Once we were children
      with a charge of such energy
          vibrating through our bodies
It was almost unbearable as we ran
      toward our visions
          impatience our constant companion
As time meandered on slow and heavy legs.

Once we were children
      running wildly across green
          landscapes and jumping ditches
             our bare feet and arms and legs
Scratched and torn with
      nary a whimper of recognition
          for we were free and bound
Only by our imaginations.

Once we were children
        with the sap of life
                brimming up and over and to
Stand in the sunshine of a new day
        was reason to weep
                from the joy of it all.

Once we were children
        eager to see who we would become
                and the memory yet lingers of
Dreams and hopes and endless possibilities
        as the anticipation of the journey
                was the best life had to give
Once, when we were children.

Gothic Fantasies

Cloudy days and
Well-dressed
Young men
Remind me of

Buildings
Tall and narrow
Red bricked
Plastered

And corniced
Columns framing
Wide
Open porches

Lakes of gray
With
Green scum and lily
Pads

Floating next to white
Swans
And woodsy
Ducks

From stands of trees
Thick and darkly
Green
Nestled below

Hills
Carved to granite
Crags
Overlooking the old

Mill
Where once the
Business
Was of powder and

Guns
And fortunes made
Shaped
A city by a

Harbor
Where Gothic
Fantasies
Live on

Tulip and Iris

Lying beside you
Shadows on the ceiling
Shifting memories of
Things once said
Thoughts once felt
Beliefs once held

"To love is to die"
Oh what a desolate
Place to lay my head
And bury my heart
What resolve there was
To never give
Never expose
Bccause to give
Is to lose
And to expose is akin to
Going unclothed on a
Trip to the South Pole

Yet here I am
Open and bare
Watching the many colors
Of Tulip and Iris sprout

From my skin
A garden of colors varied
And rich exponential in
Growth and depth of root
Energy prickles like
Shivers through my nerves
Loving it and wanting
More for finally
I am come to be

Show Me

Show me my heart
And all its feelings

Show me my blood
As it runs its quicksilver

              Path to you

Show me my soul
Aglow with all its colors

              Look at me
              A supplicant
              member of an ancient order

Awash in this symphony
That is you

              Transported

On a billowing wave
That roars its name
And sighs its purpose

              With each rise

And fall

              For it is love that rests before you

Love
Love
           and

Love again

My Mother's Garden

(October 19, 1990)

In my mother's garden
There are colors aplenty
To feed the soul
Reds and yellows and
Whites and purples and
Greens of hues too many
To claim

In my mother's garden
A hummingbird shimmers
With silken colors
As it hovers above
A hibiscus bloom
Spread wide for this
Hungry suckling

In my mother's garden
I sit on a bench of
Pristine white
My toes curled in
Short emerald grass
Like velvet on my skin

Overhead the branches
And fronds of a coconut
Palm swoop low and
Shade me from the sun

In my mother's garden
All things are like yesterday
Tomorrow is today
And my life spreads out
Like a feast of sweet
Dripping fruit falling from
Stems grown weak with
The weight of richness
So long held

In my mother's garden
I watch the birds
Flow home
A perfect V of
Fluttering wings
Unerring in their aim
Towards destiny

In my mother's garden
I sit on hallowed ground
Baring myself to
Life and its meanings
Its many wonders
Winding, binding

In my mother's garden
I watch the full moon
Rise like a silver plate
Above a nearby dark
Mountain range
Its blinding light
Serrated by the
Silhouette of palm leaves
Slowly shifting –
Its light beholds me
As it has through
Time unremembering

And in this garden
My mother's garden
I have peace and joy
In knowing love
My mother's garden
In my mother's garden

My Mother's Garden Redux

In my mother's garden
I dream of a love
That cushions me like
The deep, soft grass
Beneath my feet

In my mother's garden
I liken love to the fragrant
Satin petal of a faded lavender
Rose whose scent is yet
Undimmed
        Lean close and breathe its fullness

In my mother's garden
I raise the golden cup of a
Ripe coconut to my lips
Its juice abates the thirst
Created so long ago and so long
Denied

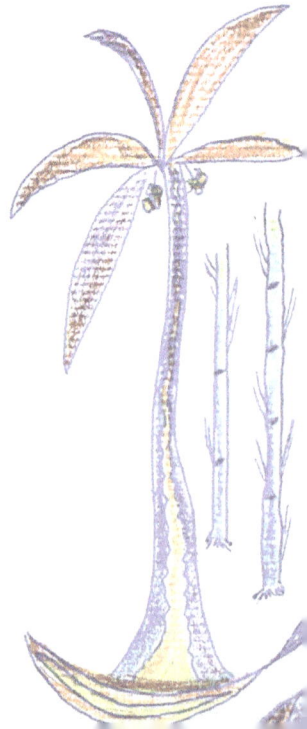

Under the quiet light of a
Half moon
I sit and wonder if the dreams
Of a lifetime can only be
Nourished ever so briefly
In the passing thoughts created here
In this garden
My mother's beautiful garden

Night Sounds

(1:49 am, Wednesday, December 21, 1994)

I thought I heard the Whistle
  of a far-off train
And winding down my Pace
  I looked and listened for its swift approach

But it must have been
  my memory
Or my heart that
  pealed its approach
For I reached my Destination
  without crossing its path

Yes, it's funny how echoes
  of things remembered
Reverb with such clarity
  through the chambers of my mind
To bring me here again
  and again
Waiting for a Train
  I think is on its way

18

But never mind
  trains have taken me places
I wanted to be and
  echoes of their Coming
Will always be met with
  sweet anticipation of
The journey to come

Boxcars
  railcars
Sleeper
  and coach
Rolling by in silver
  and blue
Brown and gray
  on and on Through
Open landscapes and
  cluttered cities
With only a blaring whistle
  to mark its coming
And a clatter of wheels
  on rails
To say
  So Long

Simple Things

What are simple things made of?
Birds on a roof
Silhouetted and dark
Skies so blue and
Day so cool
All in a line
Watchful and primed
To fly at the drop
Of a dime

What are simple things made of?
A tiny arm moving above a
Ribboned head
Waving at a delighted stranger
Peering to see more than hair
And curious eyes as the greeter's
Bus speeds away revealing nothing
But bright John Deere Yellow
Against a green day

Simple things are
A dog's tail
Black and long
Gliding along

The edge
Of a tabletop
     The tail's there - where is the dog?
     If you see a moving dog's tail but
     No dog, does the dog exist?

     What are simple things made of?
Bits and pieces of snap and whimsy
That sets me dreaming about having
The vision to see the entire thing
This mosaic I'm part of and
Walking on
Black dog's tail and birds on a
Church bearing a fluorescent cross
And little girls who wave like
Elizabeth the Second from
Her coach shining in
John Deere Yellow

Circles

*(C1992 while working at a women's
drug treatment center)*

The beat beat beat
Of the hip hop sounds
Mixes loudly with
The laughing voices
Excited and shrill
Punctuated by pauses
As cigarettes are placed
To lips and smoke
Blown into air
Brilliant with sunshine

Under skies of blue
Bleached with light
They sit in a circle –
These women –
The shape of their bonding
A union never to be forgotten
Like the stories they tell
With slaps of the knee
Waving arms and
Explosions of
Joy wafting high

The beat changes
And the rhythm
Entices one to leap about
Shoulders jerking
Dust rising
Cigarette held aloft making
Circles of smoke

She likes this music
The attention even more
During these moments when
Grace becomes her
And history leaves

In the background a woman
Pauses
Back bent
Hands still gripping
Wet clothes awash in a bucket
Her eyes on the show

Her face tells the story
Of longings to be free
But something holds her tied
Holds her wishing
somewhere apart
While laughing women
Share in the glare of moments
Suspended under a bleached sky

Freight Train Passing

(Louie Boy Redux)

Boxcars rolling by
Myths and legends of a nation
On noisy metal wheels
Louie Boy splashed in
Yellow paint on wood
Written where
By whom
For Louie

Other labels rush by in black or white
Stencil letters like bits of
Social history in the passing
One hundred years ago
Sitting a horse by a railroad
Crossing would I have seen
Boxcars labeled
Corn Syrup Sweeteners? Maybe
Caustic Soda? Possibly
Liquified Petroleum Gas?

One hundred years beyond this moment
Will freight trains still be rolling by?

But how binding of past to present
Sitting here
Sun pressing my skin
Through an open sunroof
Easy in my seat with the sound of
Clattering metal echoing
Through the years

Two

Autumn Journey

Let us dance then
You and I
To the strains of
Music haunting and
Sweet fruit dripping
Juices sticky warm
Sun pulsing heat
Drying my eyes
Blinking in hazy
Wonderment at you
There before me
Hair of gold long and
Smooth swinging
Softly to music
Low pushcart rolling
Black skin
Glistening sweat and
Dreams of cold exploding
In a tossed ball
Trees hanging low
Under weight of fresh
Fall leaves dazzling
In varied colors
Of rushing waters

Over slippery boulders
Sounds of rapid motion
A tugging rope hung
From my heart
For there you sit
Tense and serene
Oblivious of this dance
We are locked in
Haunting and blind

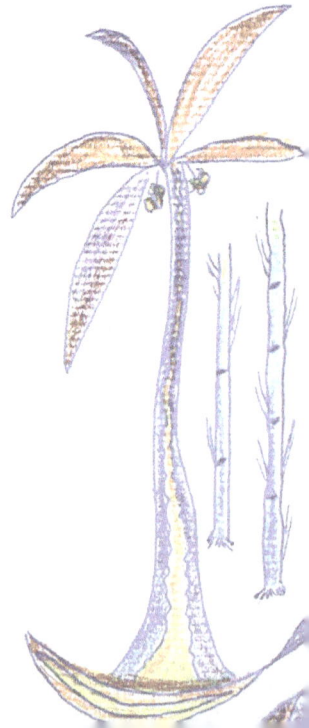

Rehearsal

I walk among candles

     to see you there

I would strip you of

     clothing and lay

You naked across this

     trodden path if only

The world would leave us unaware

      As my weight descends

To match your own and

     All lovers are mere rehearsal

For this exhibition

     We have been dancing

Forever and anon

New Haven

Rooms so bare
Rectangles of light
And space
Giving me leave
To feel my growth

Lying naked
Skin afire
Open window a
Vacuum barring
Cool slow breezes

Dreamtime comes
My stomach contracts
The pain of possibilities
A promise
A burden
Welcomed

New Haven
Opening to me
Like a book long heard of
Coming to me like
A lover kneeling
Bending, unfolding

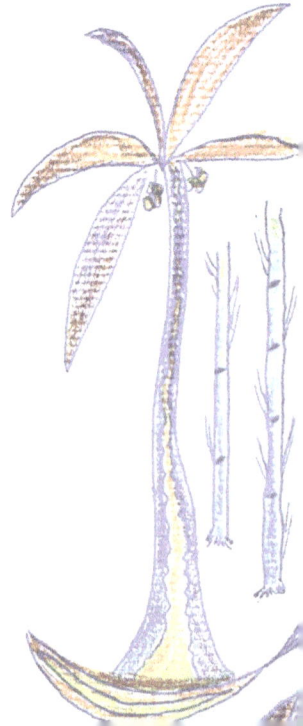

Her length on mine
Fills me with pleasure
Long suspended

Her kiss is as a whisper
Yet I am full with a
Passion long contained
And I wrap her to me with
An intent and desire for
New Haven

My dream of harmony
On a morning warm
In arms so strong

Dreams, dreams are
Always there

I cup a breast and
Sigh my fill and
Sleeping wake to
See again
New Haven New Haven
Whispers of New Haven
In arms graceful and strong

She is mine
When I dream it so
In New Haven again

June 14, 1990

Days of rain
Hold no fear
Sunshine, like birthdays,
Are always there.

Thoughts Of You

Come to me
In this home
that holds my
thoughts of you

You in this chair
By a window bright
Blue sea in the
Distance framed by
Palms thick and
Swaying
Coconuts a burnt
Yellow
Ready for the cutting

You'll sit
Head tilted back and
Hair hanging down
Eyes closed as you
Enjoy the beauty
Of seamless sounds
The distant drone
Of water in motion
Air moving along the

Edges of leaves
Birds calling their
News to each other
It all becomes one

I shall sit at your
feet and speak you
poetry from countries
we have yet to know
and poets who call
for an ear to listen

I will wrap you
To me as the sun
Falls away and our
Aspects change one
To the other
Wrap you to me and
Inhale the heat of
Your skin
Feel the texture of
Your bones beneath
And shiver at the
Softness of your lips
Against my skin as
You murmur in tones
Distinctive in its
Cadence
My name paired with
"I love you"

Come to me in life
My darling
For hopes and wishes
Are too controlled
Too exact
And life is so gloriously
An inexact science
That calls out again
And again
Come to me

Once Known

(December 13, 1978)

Once known
Never forgotten
Through all the
Years
The force stays
Never obvious
Never obscure

Until all at once
It rises
Calling for
Instant care

And as its
Power and all
Its meaning
Thrusts its way
Into the conscious
Feelings
You know
You must obey
Its call

Or else forever
Be lost

Lost
And never knowing
Why

Once known
Never forgotten
Is you, my love
You came to me
When I was Searching
For what I did Not know
You came and I Knew
that you Were there
But never once
Did I acknowledge
That you were part
Of what I had been Searching for
Part of
Not all

But
Once known
Never forgotten

So Long Now

So long now
Since I was here

So far away
My thoughts have been

Should I return
                To be with you?

Still, I'll go
The places of whim

Stay with me
                And never leave

Whims and fancies
Are not for you

                I am the one
The only one

Again

(November 17, 1994)

Through the trees and
Down the tracks

Darkness a canvas
Behind and above

Love moves with a
Clatter and a rattle

Noisy in its passing
Tardy in its coming

Splinters of broken light
Bounce from its wheels

Its sides
Its many protrusions
Bristling fierce and soft

Soft as your voice
Brushing my ear
        There

Once again
　　　　There

Your whistle echoes
From the darkness

And I am still
　　　　Again
Waiting for you there

Waiting as the ground
Vibrates beneath my feet

Then stills
Steadies

To reveal
　　　　Silence
Then
Whispers and warm breath
Against my skin
For ever and ever
　　　　Again

Night Dark Streets

Somewhere along
This night dark street
Of twisted branches and
Hanging moss
You wait for me.

My body a shadowy
Form that stretches
For yours
Anxiety suspended
Passion unending.

I think of you in frozen moments
The glance of passion
The touch of warmth
The look of your arms
Glowing in the burning sun
The veins blue atop your
Tapered hands

I wanted you then
And so very many times
Before
But that is not
For me, I thought, never for me.

Yet passion or be it
Obsession
Responds not to words
Of restraint and
I walk beside you
Cautious in my guilt
For wanting what I
Will not have
Obeying the dictates of
My honor
Yet flying free in
My need to have
A love which has
No logic but yet is.

My love, if I should leave
To be with another
Know always that for me you
Lit a shaded candle which
Warmed me inside
Unlike any phases of
the sun outside.

Now as I think
And as I dream
Once more of you
I want you and hope that
You will also want me for

Along these night dark streets
Of twisted branches and
Hanging moss
I wait for you to
Come to me.

Three

Gentle Me

Gentle me my darling
The dreams do come again
They come in darkest
Brightest night
In unrisen dawn
In sun-filled day
Filling my mind
With wonder
And my needs to dust

I hate to wake and
Face the day
All its nonsense
I do abhor
Yet in sleep there
Is no rest
Only torment of
Images not understood

So, gentle me my
Darling
The dreams do come
Again

44

Goodbye Love

Goodbye love
I hardly knew
You were here

Why didn't you
Call to me in
A voice urgent
With your need
For me

Goodbye love
Why do you
Leave me now?

Didn't I show
You every way
I knew
That you were
The only one
Who made me feel?

Goodbye love
I won't shed
My tears
For what I
Never had

I was yours
You were never mine
So
Goodbye my love

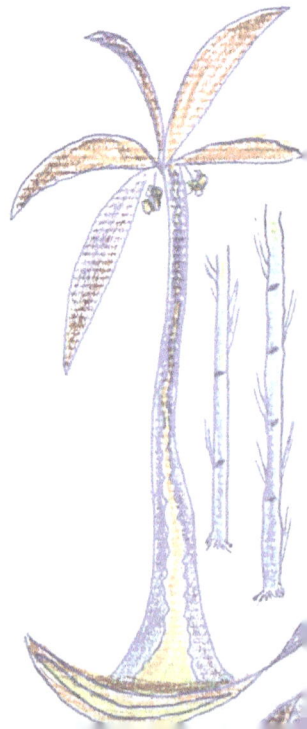

The Day Is Done

My love
The day is done

      Like love that
      Wraps around me
      Then loosens in
      Sudden flight

The day is done
And love goes on

My Shining One

Tears of sadness
      Yet to come
Tears for you
So far away
Yet I see you
      As I saw you then
Tall and straight
Calm and dear
My protector
My savior
      My shining one
Come to take me
Away from pain
Away from bewilderment
      Memories are forever
Life is now
Death is when
Love is life

Tales Of Old

Tales of death
To make me know
It could next be me

Tales of death
To make me follow
The path prescribed

Tales of death
To change what is

"Look at this," they say,
"It could be you any day now!"

Yes, any day
And any day
No matter what
Paths I follow

The one directed
By inner voices
Or those of
Other voices

Tales of death are
With me always
Companions known
In a life of change

In Passing

(Written at 17 when my brother, Donald, was dying)

Will you remember me
When I am gone
And this we know
Is exchanged for another

Will anything be left
To say I was here
Or just another name
Among countless many

Who can explain this
Ambition that hopes
To be the sun among stars
To shine on after

We do not know
We cannot say
But life is the memory of minds
So, will you remember me

Cry If You Will

(March 8, 1982)

I saw the present
Anticipated the future
Rejected both
Wanting only the past
                    The beautiful past
With everything
Made perfect by
The fading passage of
Time

No rough edges
No sparks of discontent
Only the pastel colors
Of sight gone blurred
                    That time is over
Cry if you will for
Days never to be
               Again
Cry if you will
For the aging of
Your only body

Those times remain
Only on the shelves of your
                    Mind
Getting richer
More beautiful
In time

Look to the future
Live for the present
If you would be happy

It is the future and
Your present which
Continues to make
Those memories you
Treasure
It's up to you
If they be perfect

Cry if you will

Mirror Mirror

Mirror mirror
On the wall
What do we look
For after all
When your surface
Do us reflect
In silvered images
Of life's tender flesh

With our eyes we
Search
To find a truth eluded
In a world of three
Dimension

Closer we lean
Examining pores and
The hair they sprout
Amazed at the life
That exists even
While our lives
Seemingly go nowhere

The eyes it's said
Hold all truths
The secret is to know
The formula that interprets

Mirror mirror
On the wall
What's the secret of it all?

When I'm gone
You will remain
Your silvered surface
Giving truth in two
Dimensions
While eyes meet eyes
In search of secrets

Mind flutters

Do you feel my breath
Upon your body
As your soul I do explore
Can you see the sweat
Upon my skin
As my mind flutters
Lose all control

When you walked into my life
You broke the bonds
Which kept me tight
And now I am out of control
Losing myself to you
Releasing all face values
I had taken to keep

Mind flutters
Mind flutters
Strobing thoughts of
You and me
The heat is burning
And we're turning
Over and over
Out of control

My breathing slows
My mind retreats
To that place of distance
And peace

The flesh cools
My mind goes cold
As the future of my dreams
Moves swiftly away

Oh, it's cold where I am
Won't someone come
Take me to a warm place

Now you say you love me
Now you say you want me
Now you say you need me
What is that to change
The warm place you offer
Demands a price
And a sucker like me
Is just the one to pay

Do you feel me?
Do you breathe me?
I am you!
Don't you know?

For Cassie

It's one in the morning
As the deep echo
Of the train whistle
Sharp
Rolling wheels a receding
Thunder
In the night
Wrapped closely around me
Snuggled amongst my quilts
And sheets
Pillow a haven for the
Vessel of my thoughts
And memories of a
Child
Sweet and golden
Like a vision of another
From long ago who
Looked to me from
Mirrors and rippled
Ponds and softly whispered
"I am coming and who will you be?
I long to know you as you will be,
So I'll walk the waters and
Soar the air and see you

In that place of bright
Light
And endless vista
When our time has come
To truly know."

I smile to think how
That will be for I
Have seen it and so
I know I'll always
Be you as you are me.
The breath of our lives
Has made it so.

Miss P

Seven o'clock
She passed on
No watching eyes
To see her final sigh

Seven o'clock
She passed on
It's not real
Has she really gone?
No feeling
No tears
Nothing

Seven o'clock
She passed on
Long ago she walked
Young, strong, beautiful
Laughter on her lips
Smile on her face

Seven o'clock
She passed on

I cry.

Pearl Harbour (relic of old Kingston)

(Written Circa 1972)

Grinning faces
Staring eyes
Voices crying out
Pearl Harbour!
Hey, Pearl Harbour
Yu so famous
But mi never
See yu before
Hear yu sell
Yuself to any man.

Pearl Harbour!
Hey, Pearl Harbour
Yu must did look
Good as a young
wo – man.
See yu now
Wha happen to yu?
Dragging yu foot
And making mi

Feel sorry fi yu
Eh, Pearl Harbour!

Pearl Harbour!
Hey! Pearl Harbour
Age catch up wid yu
De man dem now
Only laugh and jeer
As yu walk upon
Your famous way
Fame comes youth goes
What price fame.
Hey, Pearl,
Take care, yu hear!

The All

This is all we have
   All we will ever know

All else are dreams
   Perchance even fantasies

But still the truth
   I buried

And lines unhurried
   Wrote

For the end
   Is the end

So why not let it be

Four

What Is Life

What is this life
If not with you
What is this world
If not for you

> *The mornings*
> *The noons*
> *The evenings*
> *And darkest*
> *Latest*
> *Of nights*
> *Are life's gifts*
> *Made clear*
> *Because…you*

What is life,
I ask,
If not seen
In your eyes
Aglow with love
For me

Frisson

Out from the dark
Words came to me
In the silver glow
Of a winter moon

Pointless pointless life
It sometimes seems
Waiting here for a
Burst that rarely comes

Gathering covers around
My body for warmth
And solace
Reaching for that
Glittering swift gift
A frisson across my mind

Dreaming

I would hold you now
Your weight sinking
Me into the feathery
Arms of these pillows
Your lips on mine
Your hands –
Beauty that sparks
My desire –
Touching lightly
To call me home

Oh, how I want you
As I have no other
You call to me from
A place deep within
Your voice remembered
From a dream I
Thought I lived
So familiar was this place
That welcomed and
Embraced promises
Of pleasure never-ending
In the glance of your

Eyes
The curl of your
Lips
An expression that pulls
On the bonds which
Weaves from you to me

Oh, Woman

Oh woman
    Thru all the ages
Your life was fashioned
    Simply for this
For this you hoped
    For this you looked
If there is more
    It is yet to come
Search with me
    In times to come
Together the light
    May be at hand
Illusions are not
    What we seek

Words Of Love

Words of love we speak
              into the night darkness of sleep
Tight and close our arms enfold
              as gentle whispers slowly flow
Along the twisting path
              connecting you to me in
This bond invisible and secure
              which pulls us back yet again
And reminds me what joy
              there is in making love with
Words and eyes
              and losing you is again a
Beginning of the journey to
              find you anew once more

My Valentine 1997

Show me my heart
And all its feelings
Show me my blood
As it runs its quicksilver
Path to you

Show me my soul
In all its colors
That deepen and glow
With knowledge of you

Look at me
A supplicant -- member of
An ancient order -- awash
In this symphony
That is you in all
Your supple grace
Transported on a
Billowing wave
That roars its name
And sighs its purpose
With each rise
And fall

For it is love that
Rests before you
Love Love and Love
Again

My Valentine 1999

I am reminded as
I sit here thinking
of you
how fearful I become
when you prepare to
leave
All the fears of my
life
coalesce to a
white hot point of
panic and I am
swept into the cauldron
and forced to swim
again

It is you I swim to
my love
In these moments
when darkness
threatens me and
the pulse of blood
through my veins is

an escalating roar like
the vertiginous waterfall
I am being swept toward

I swim to you
when intellect leaves and
I am again just a
frightened child
in a world
gone gone gone
away
leaving me alone in
the crashing silence

You I swim to
because God is good
and the universe is a
budding yellow rose
waiting to
release its fragrance
upon us and the
gifts of life are
numerous and endless

And as I see you there
tears break within me
because loving you
is the best of me
and your love
is the water
and the sun
the moon and
the stars

and all the planets
in between and I
raise my face
I raise my arms
to the crashing sky
and I say again
and yet again
Thank you

This Birth Day

(January 16, 1999)

On this day
This day of beginnings
My love's voice
Reaches to me like
The seductive call
Of the siren from
The wave-washed
Rock
Reaches to me and
Calls me near
Nearer and so
Close with promises
Of warmth and
Light
And the beating of
Her heart next to
Mine
Oh, how could I
Refuse when my
Whole life leads me
To this and you
For the beating of
Your heart is the

76

Echo I have heard
All my years
And the mountains
I have gazed upon
I have done so
With your eyes
And the aching
Gnawing longing
I have felt is
You longing for
Me
For I have known
You ever
And ever have I
Felt you near
And longed to
Touch you there
Upon your wave washed
Rock
Just out of reach
But my boat
Has brought me
Here and my eyes
That have been
Yours
That have been
Mine
Gaze now only
Upon love and
Now
As I lay me down
I look to you and
I am filled
Filled with you

My Love

Across the land
a continent away
on the shores of
another ocean
my love speaks
to me and the
shimmering cord
of our love vibrates
and crackles with
its energy speeding
through its length

"Hi, honey!" she says
and I am calmed
and filled to rest
another day

Curling Gently

My love lays beside me
      the left of my right
The front of my
      back
My profile and my
      full frontal
The fruit of my
      burgeoning heart
The core of my
      dreams
Warm and soft
      she curls gently around
My heart

Lost

I am a hibernating cub
curled into your warmth
The cold like clutching fingers
at my exposed skin
My nipples hard and raw
painful in their stiffness
Crying for heat
crying for warmth
Snuggling closer and
sinking in
Lost in your softness

Slowly

Sliding slowly
      to another day
     Peace and joy
in memories of this

This day of beauty
      this day of joy
     This day of love
and being loved

Be Of Good Heart

Be of good heart
My mother
Love is with you
Always

I have loved you
Since that day
Of tears and fear
When standing
Lost and alone
I saw you in
The distance

You came and
Took my hand
           "You're coming home with me"
You said

Home since then
Has always been
Where you are

Through my childhood
You gave me love
You gave me laughter
In my youth
You gave me love
You gave me laughter

Through it all you
Also taught me
To care for my
Fellow man
You taught me
Honesty
Respect
Loyalty
And sympathy
That love of all
Is love of god

Yes, my mother
We have laughed
And we have cried
We have been angry
We have been sad
Yet, through it all,
There was love

And as I sit here
So many miles
Away
I look at your image
And am reminded

Once again
Of the beauty that
Is you

Be of good heart
My mother
Love is constant
Love is good
Love accepts the
Bad times as a prelude
To the good

Love is with you
Always
In the love I
Have for you

Ivy, young

Woman hurrying across the street
Away from my oncoming car
Big hips swaying
Long legs striding
With confidence pure
Reminding me of
Ivy,
Young and strong
Tall and straight
Moving through
Obstacles
Hard
Her pain expressed in
Late night tears
Beside a window dark
Observed in quiet fear
By me, the child
Cloaked in my attitude
Of sleep
Yet wide awake
And wondering what could
Cause this woman
Forceful and proud
To break stride and whimper

As she observed the images
Of her fears illuminated in
That window's view

Ivy, young and strong
Soft and fearful
Lives in my memory
Like slow breaths
That whisper
Of forever
And ever

Miles to Go

(on Joan turning 60, January 16, 2011)

A bike ride on a Sunday morning
Saturday dinner with friends
A late night snuggle with love
Warmth on a chilly January night

Memories of recent days spent
With your greatest creations
Young men of exception
Warm and loving, admirers of
Their Mama Dutz - a nonsensical
Name of their youth that lives on

Sunrise over Lake Virginia
Runners breath like billowing smoke
Heat scything through cold
Miles behind you and miles to go
The pleasure unending

The years rush in
Time known if not understood
You meet it smiling
Looking forward running onward
Determined to experience all it brings

Work hard, love deep
Never give up
Challenges sought and life met
Thoughts of Jane and Stuart
And their images in you

My love my Joan
You are you are
The one the only one
My sun my moon my starry sky
My warmth my dreams
My life's imaginings
You are love
You are life itself

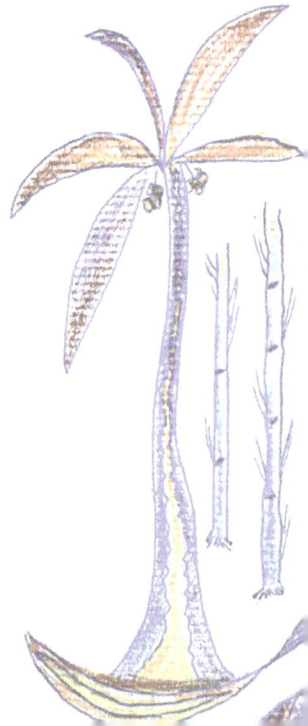

Scotty Loves Lynn

(February 14, 1994)

Scotty loves Lynn
Are words quickly read
On a highway overpass
The sprayed black letters
Snaking along a
Concrete wall

Scotty loves Lynn
Does Lynn love Scotty?
Or is it again,
Once again,
Love unnurtured
Love unfed
Flames sustained by
The air of life
But never growing
Stronger its
Light dimly beaming

Scotty loves Lynn
What hope there is
What confidence in the
Future to so proclaim

I love these two
Love their love and
The possibility of it
This call to love
This shout of love
This declaratory call
Weaves through me
With tenderness and
Joy as I drive
The straight highway

Scotty loved Lynn
On February 14, 1994
And I hope
He
Still
Does

Five

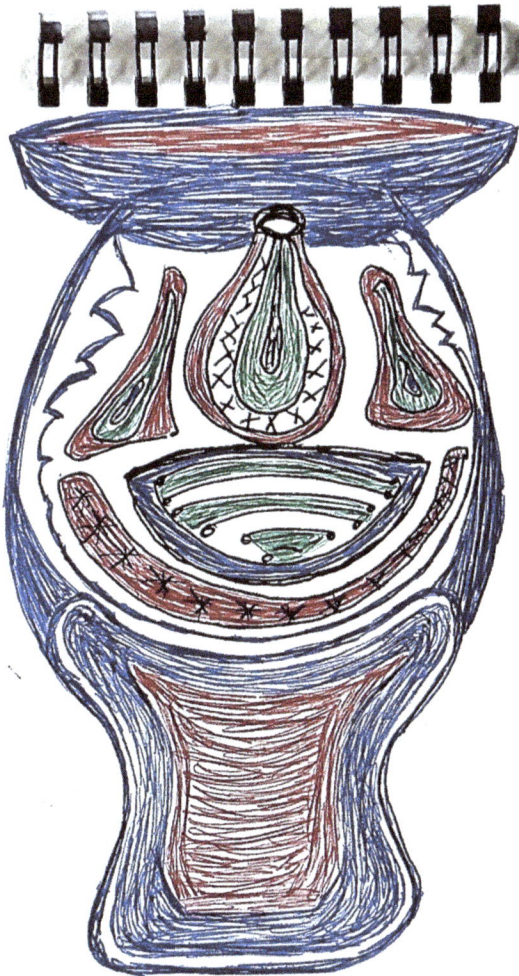

A Writer's Dream

Here I sit
      Pen poised to fit
As voices whirl
      And color's swirl
Across a blank page

Alive
Alive
It calls to me
Will I answer?

Long time gone
Are words that
Come to me
As I dream of flying
To the one place
I can live to be a hundred
With friends I love like you

It was a death of dreams
And perhaps a sort of
                    Love
Found in the golden light
                    Of noon
Next to someone gently
                    Mine
For just that time

Epilogue

Guerrilla Man

(Circa 1980 for a college writing class)

I heard he died last Saturday noon
Killed by a shotgun blast as
Fruit he bought by a wayside stand.

Seems the man didn't like his looks
Nor his car
Or the way he spoke.

Neil, he tried to beat down the price
On a bag oranges
But didn't know golden fruit
Would spill his blood
To be dried by old gold sun.

Seems the man then shot up the car
(stupid jack, he coulda driven it off)
Then took to bush screaming he'd
Rid the land of all 'talists.

In days to come
From the trees he'll aim and
Bring them down for crows
To feast.

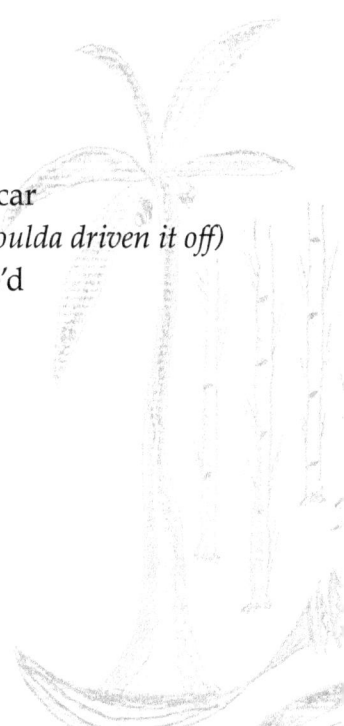

No more fancy cars to ride beside
The barefoot man.

No more shacks being washed
Down river by friendly drizzles.

No more walking through garbage
To find an evening meal.

No. No more!

In the vision of a
Perfect creation
He'll come with his people behind
A gun in hand 'stead of flute
Down from the mountains
Out from the trees
Cheers and tears and laughter
And music
Marking the way to the sea
Where in face of the horizon
A new future he'll proclaim.

Yes
I heard he died
Last Saturday noon
Killed by a shotgun blast
In face of the horizon.

About the Author

YCT Vassel was born and raised in Kingston, Jamaica, and completed two years of National Youth Service with the government's then Agency for Public Information (now Jamaica Information Service, JIS) before attending college in the USA. Work as a print journalist in Connecticut and Florida was followed by stints in the areas of substance abuse, retail, college communications and writing professor, an agency spokesperson for Florida's state government, and recruitment and organizing for a Washington, DC, transportation lobbying firm. For the last 12 years she has guided others in writing and compiling their life stories.

Publication Acknowledgment

"Pearl Harbour (relic of Old Kingston)" first appeared in: *Groundswell*, a literary publication of the University of Bridgeport, CT. (1980)

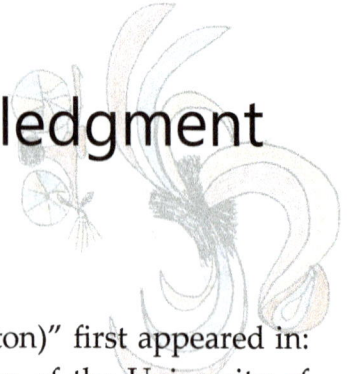

www.ingramcontent.com/pod-product-compliance
Lightning Source LLC
LaVergne TN
LVHW022012080426
835513LV00009B/686